Food JOKES to Tickle Your FUNNY BONE

Linda Bozzo

Enslow Elementary
an imprint of

Enslow Publishers, Inc.
40 Industrial Road
Box 398
Berkeley Heights, NJ 07922
USA

http://www.enslow.com

To all of the people who make me laugh!

Enslow Elementary, an imprint of Enslow Publishers, Inc.

Enslow Elementary® is a registered trademark of Enslow Publishers, Inc.

Library of Congress Cataloging-in-Publication Data

Bozzo, Linda.

    Food jokes to tickle your funny bone / Linda Bozzo.

        p. cm. — (Funny bone jokes)

    Includes bibliographical references and index.

    Summary: "Includes jokes, limericks, knock-knock jokes, tongue twisters, and fun facts about different fruits, vegetables, chocolate, popcorn, ice cream, and more, and describes how to write your own knock-knock jokes and how to create your own joke book"—Provided by publisher.

    ISBN 978-0-7660-3541-6

    1. Food—Juvenile humor. I. Title.

    PN6231.F66B69 2010

    818'.602—dc22

                          2010006171

ePUB ISBN 978-1-4645-0316-0

PDF ISBN 978-1-4646-0316-7

Printed in the United States of America

122011 Lake Book Manufacturing, Inc., Melrose Park, IL

10 9 8 7 6 5 4 3 2

Contents

Fresh Strawberries

Did you hear the one about the strawberry jam?

It's berry funny!

Knock, Knock!

Who's there?

Olive

Olive who?

Olive around the corner on Strawberry Lane.

What kind of fruit do you feed a scarecrow?

"Straw" berries.

Where do strawberries play music?

At a jam session.

How do you make a strawberry swirl?

Send it to ballet school!

How do you make a strawberry shake?

Put it in the fridge!

Why do elephants paint their toenails red?

So they can hide in a strawberry patch.

DID YOU KNOW?

Strawberry plants can be grown in a garden or in a pot. It is best to buy a plant in the early spring. There are many different kinds of strawberries. Some strawberries are large and some are small. Some are sweeter than others.

IT'S TRUE.

Knock, Knock!

Who's there?

Maida

Maida who?

Maida strawberry cake for you.

I know a lady from Ferrys
Who swallowed the pits from some cherries.
They grew into three
Big cherry trees,
So now she eats only strawberries.

Each time you see this squiggly box, it is a tongue twister! Try saying it five times fast!

Sheep shouldn't sip strawberry shakes on a small ship.

There once was a fellow who tried
To grow gardens of berries inside.
But there was no sun,
So he only grew one,
And the fellow just sat down and cried.

When is a berry not a berry? The answer is, when it is a strawberry. This bright red fruit with a green cap is not a true berry like blueberries and cranberries. The strawberry plant is a member of the rose family. They are easy to grow. That is why they are found in many gardens.

IT'S TRUE.

Knock, Knock!

Who's there?

Berry

Berry who?

Berry nice to meet you.

Frank finished Franny's fat-free fruity float.

Delicious Apples

What's worse than finding a worm in your apple?

Finding half a worm.

What do you get when you stuff a turkey with apples?

An apple gobbler.

Eight eager apes ate eight apples.

Knock, Knock!

Who's there?

Eye

Eye who?

Eye know you took a bite out of my apple!

DID YOU KNOW?

The first apples grown in the United States were planted by the Pilgrims in Massachusetts. You might recognize the name Johnny Appleseed. His real name was John Chapman. He was called Johnny Appleseed because he was known for traveling across the Ohio Valley carrying bags of apple seeds. He planted seeds and grew apples as he traveled west to spread trees so settlers could have apples to eat.

IT'S TRUE.

Ohio Valley

What does an apple have that no other fruit has?

Apple seeds.

Knock, Knock!

Who's there?

Ben

Ben who?

Why did the apple stop running?

It ran out of juice.

Ben out picking apples.

There was a young fellow who thought
So much that he always forgot
That he hid all his fruit
In the sole of his boot
Until it started to smell a lot!

What place do worms
like to visit the most?

The Big Apple.

What kind of apple
isn't an apple?

A pineapple.

FUN FACTS

IT'S TRUE.

What is your favorite fruit? Most people enjoy sinking their teeth into a sweet, juicy apple. This healthy snack starts out as a small seed that grows into a tree. Apple trees are grown on farms known as orchards. In spring, the apple tree is covered with white blossoms that will be pollinated by insects. Then, the blossoms fall off and apples begin to grow in their place throughout the summer. The apples are usually fully grown, ripened, and ready to be picked in autumn.

Knock, Knock!

Who's there?

Owl

Owl who?

Owl be baking apple pies all day.

Peggy picked plenty of pretty apples.

There once was a boy from Pete
Who would never eat anything sweet.
Instead of some cake,
He would rather he take
Some juicy green apples to eat.

Seeds sell slowly on sale at the seed shop.

③ Everyone's Favorite... Chocolate

Why did the donut go to the dentist?

To get a chocolate filling.

How do you say chocolate in French?

Chocolate in French.

Which candy can't get anywhere on time?

Choco-late!

Everyone loves chocolate! It might surprise you to know that chocolate is made from the seeds of the cacao (kah KOW) tree. The seeds are dried and processed. They are crushed, mixed, and rolled. Finally, they are molded by machines to make sweet candy.

Knock, Knock!

Who's there?

Water

Water who?

Water you doing with my hot chocolate?

A mouse once said to a cat,
"It's chocolate that's making me fat."
So the cat fed him more
Until he was sure
The mouse looked more like a rat.

What do you get if you cross milk, chocolate, and a scary movie?

A chocolate milk shake!

Why did the monster get fired from his job at the candy store?

He kept biting the heads off the chocolate bunnies!

What do good bakers earn?

Brownie points.

How much cake could a baker bake if a baker could bake chocolate cake?

FUN FACTS

Today, chocolate can be found in many sweets like cookies and cakes. But did you know that the first chocolate was a bitter drink? Sugar was added to make it sweet. Spices were added for flavor. At one time, because cacao and sugar cost too much, only those with money could afford to drink chocolate. Over time, the process of making chocolate has become faster and easier.

IT'S TRUE.

A hungry young man who would eat
Chocolate in all kinds of heat
Would always get sick
Whenever he licked
The chocolate he dripped on his feet.

Charlie quietly clapped while Chris quickly kept chewing chocolate-covered cherries.

Knock, Knock!

Who's there?

Shirley

Shirley who?

Shirley you have some chocolate!

Spread the Butter 4

How can you tell that an elephant has been in your refrigerator?

Look for footprints in the butter.

The batter better be better before Betty bakes banana bread.

What did the butter say to the duck?

Nothing. Butter can't talk!

Why did Silly Sally feed the cow money?

So she could get rich milk.

Butter is a solid fat made from milk, cream, or both. Solid fats come from animal products like cow's milk. Solid fats stay solid at room temperature. It is important to know that fats, such as oils, nuts, and butter, are not a food group. That does not mean they are not important. Fats help kids grow and give them energy. Our bodies need fat but only in small amounts.

IT'S TRUE.

Why did the boy throw a stick of butter out of the window?

He wanted to see a butterfly.

What do you say to a sick dairy farmer?

Feel butter!

Knock, Knock!

Who's there?

Owl

Owl who?

Owl get the butter.

When does a batter beat batter?

When a baseball player makes pancakes.

Knock, Knock!

Who's there?

Justin

Justin who?

Justin time for pancakes with butter!

What weighs more, a pound of butter or a pound of feathers?

They both weigh a pound.

There once was a snowman named Joe
Who had a snow girlfriend named Flo.
They both really felt
They might someday melt
Into butter instead of snow.

FUN FACTS

Most people keep their butter in the refrigerator. When kept in the refrigerator, butter gets hard. This makes it difficult to spread. Butter can actually be kept at room temperature for many days without going bad. Whether on your counter or in your refrigerator, butter needs to be kept in a butter keeper. Butter easily picks up odors and flavors from other foods. In other words, if it is not covered, your butter will "stink."

IT'S TRUE.

There once was a boy named Ted
Who had a best friend named Fred
Who ate so much butter
He looked like his mother,
So he started to eat plain bread instead.

Knock, Knock!

Who's there?

Butter

Butter who?

Butter let me in!

Excellent Eggs ⑤

Did you hear the joke about the 50-year-old egg?

It's a very old yolk.

Why did the chicken lay an egg?

Because if she dropped it, it would break!

FUN FACTS

The color of yolk depends on what the hen eats. Egg yolks can vary in color from deep yellow to almost colorless. The yolk is where most of the egg's vitamins and minerals are found. Did you know that a mother hen turns her eggs over about fifty times each day? That's no yolk! Turning the eggs keeps the yolk from sticking to the sides of the shell.

IT'S TRUE.

If a rooster laid a white egg and a brown egg, what kinds of chicks would hatch?

None. Roosters don't lay eggs!

Why were the naughty eggs sent out of the class?

For playing practical yolks!

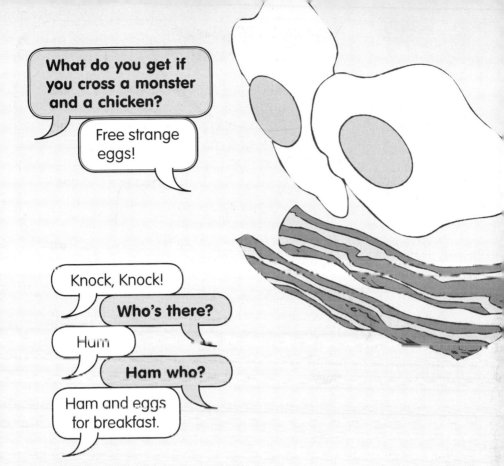

What do you get if you cross a monster and a chicken?

Free strange eggs!

Knock, Knock!

Who's there?

Ham

Ham who?

Ham and eggs for breakfast.

FUN FACTS

IT'S TRUE.

Eggs are rich in protein. That is why they are included in the meat, poultry, fish, dry beans, and nuts category of the food pyramid. But have you ever wondered why some eggs are brown and some are white? The color of an egg's shell depends on the type of hen that laid the egg. Hens with white feathers and white earlobes lay eggs with white shells. Hens with red feathers and red earlobes lay eggs with brown shells.

Knock, Knock!

Who's there?

Egg

Egg who?

It's egg-stremely cold out here! Let me in!

There once was an egg with a smell
That rose from a crack in its shell.
A stench worse than his toes,
Sam plugged up his nose
And to the egg he said a farewell.

How do ghosts like their eggs?

Terri-fried!

Sweet Honey 6

Knock, Knock!

Who's there?

Beehive

Beehive who?

Beehive yourself or you'll get in trouble!

Where would you find a bee?

At the start of the alphabet!

FUN FACTS

IT'S TRUE.

Honey is a sweet, sugary material made by bees from the nectar, a sweet liquid, of flowers. Honey is one of the world's oldest foods. Bees have been making honey for at least 150 million years. Did you know that honey was found in King Tut's tomb and it was still edible? That's right. Honey is the only food that does not spoil. It is also the only food that contains everything you need to stay alive, even water.

FUN FACTS IT'S TRUE.

Honey can be found in different flavors and colors. The darker the honey the stronger the taste it will have. Honey is often added to sweeten drinks or food. Some people spread honey on bread. Some use honey to bake. But honey has other uses as well. Honey has been known to soothe a sore throat or even quiet a cough.

What goes z-z-u-b, z-z-u-b?

A bee flying backward.

If you were a bee what kind of bee would you be?

Why did the bee dance on top of the honey jar?

It said, "Twist to open."

There once was a poor old man
Who thought of a really good plan.
He tried to sell honey
So he could make money,
But away from the bees he ran.

27

Three bees in
three trees.

What does a bee wear
when he goes jogging?

A swarm-up suit.

There once was a girl name Marie
Who was known as the city's queen bee.
She would buzz all about
While the people would shout,
"She's as sweet as honey could be."

Why do bees hum?

Because they don't
know the words!

Corny Popcorn 7

Peggy passes popped party popcorn.

Knock, Knock!

Who's there?

Arthur

Arthur who?

Arthur any healthy snacks left?

What did one corncob say to another?

"Aw, shucks!"

There once was a girl named Jenny
Who had just one last penny.
She used it to buy
Popcorn for a guy,
And then she didn't have any.

Scientists believe the first popcorn was made in Mexico thousands of years ago. The Aztec Indians not only ate popcorn, but they also used it for decoration. Popcorn became very popular in the United States in the late 1800s. Vendors could be found on the streets, in parks, or at carnivals and fairs selling popcorn.

IT'S TRUE.

How many ears of corn could you eat on an empty stomach?

Just one, after that your stomach isn't empty anymore.

Corn grows close in close corn rows.

Why did the cornstalk
get mad at the farmer?

He kept pulling its ears.

Knock, Knock!

Who's there?

Ears

Ears who?

Ears of corn.

There was an old man from Nook
Who loved to cook from his book.
But corn he could not
Keep inside of the pot,
So cooking classes he took.

What do they serve
for lunch in an office?

Corn on the job.

Popcorn is one of the world's oldest snacks. Have you ever wondered what makes popcorn pop? Popcorn is made out of certain corn kernels that have more water. When a popcorn kernel gets hot enough, the water makes steam. The steam causes the kernel to explode. The kernel turns itself inside out and the popcorn is popped!

If potatoes have eyes and corn has ears, what do peas have?

Each other!

What did Baby Corn say to Ma Corn?

Where's Pop Corn?

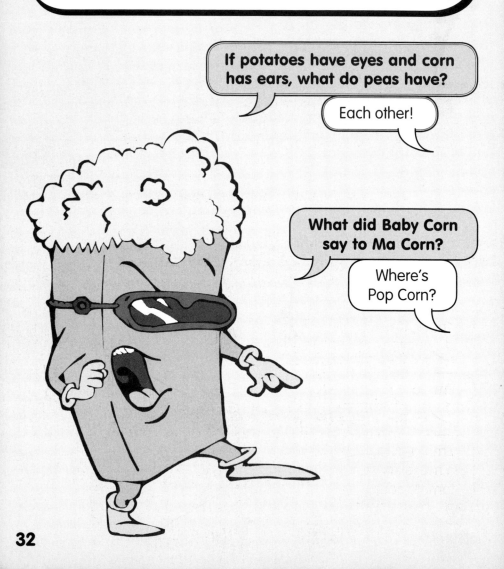

Tomatoes

How do you fix a broken pizza?

With tomato paste.

Joe mows rows where tomatoes grow.

Why did the tomato go out with the zucchini?

Because he couldn't find a date.

Knock, Knock!

Who's there?

Emma

Emma who?

Emma going to make some tomato soup.

FUN FACTS

IT'S TRUE.

Have your parents ever told you not to play with your food? They certainly would not approve of you throwing it. What if you were at the La Tomatina Festival in Spain? Every year, on the last Wednesday in August, the world's biggest tomato fight takes place at the festival. The tomato fight starts at noon and lasts a little more than an hour. One of the rules is that the tomatoes must be crushed before throwing them. This is so no one will get hurt.

If your dog's down, what's your cat?

Catsup.

Two ton trucks trucked two tons of tomatoes.

Knock, Knock!

Who's there?

Sid

Sid who?

Sid down and eat spaghetti with tomato sauce.

There was an old lady from Droop
Who found a prize on her stoop.
She suspected a dog
Because it looked like a log.
Just kidding, the prize was tomato soup.

Knock, Knock!

Who's there?

Catsup

Catsup who?

Catsup in the tree!

Why is a tomato the exact opposite of a traffic light?

You must wait for the tomato to turn from green to red and the traffic light to turn from red to green.

What did one hamburger say to another?

"You go ahead and I'll ketchup!"

People once thought tomatoes were poisonous if they were eaten. They were grown to be used as decorations. We now know that tomatoes are a delicious fruit eaten as a vegetable. Tomatoes can be found in many dishes. They add taste to salads, sandwiches, and sauces. Tomatoes can be eaten cooked or raw. They are one of the few foods that taste great from a can or fresh. **IT'S TRUE.**

A sniffly young man named Steve
Would wipe his nose on his sleeve.
Then he finally found out
Without any doubt
That the tomatoes were making him sneeze.

Why did the tomatoes have to leave the factory?

They got canned.

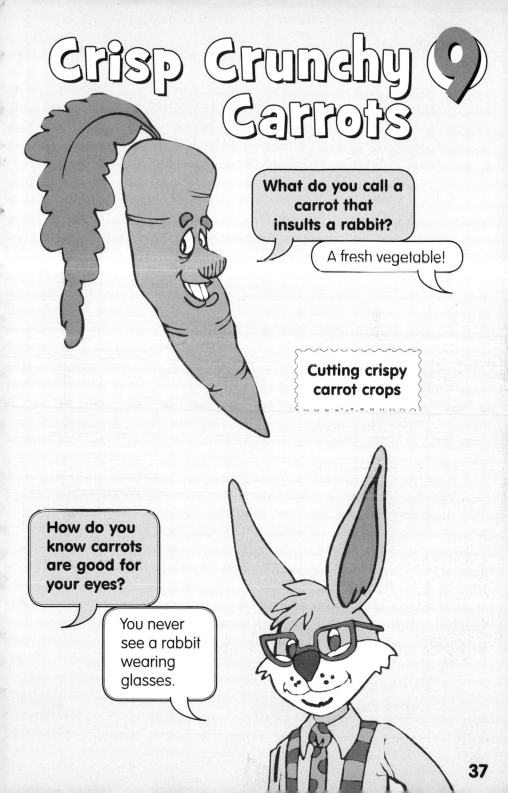

Crisp Crunchy Carrots 9

What do you call a carrot that insults a rabbit?

A fresh vegetable!

Cutting crispy carrot crops

How do you know carrots are good for your eyes?

You never see a rabbit wearing glasses.

FUN FACTS

Today, carrots can be found in many colors including orange, white, red, purple, black, and yellow. Orange carrots are the most popular. The carrot is a root vegetable that grows underground. Its green leaves grow above the ground. Carrots are rich in vitamins and high in minerals. The best part is they are available all year long.

IT'S TRUE.

How can you catch a rabbit?

Hide under a bush and make noise like a carrot!

Why do rabbits eat raw carrots?

They don't know how to cook them.

Crispy colorful carrot chips

There was a rabbit from Loop
Whose mother liked to make soup.
But carrots were not
What she put in the pot.
This rabbit preferred chicken soup.

Knock, Knock!

Who's there?

Norma Lee

Norma Lee
who?

Norma Lee
I don't eat
raw carrots.

What did one
carrot say to the
other carrot?

Nothing. Carrots
can't talk!

Knock, Knock!

Who's there?

Peace

Peace who?

Peace and
carrots!

The father bunny named Jack,
Of his bunnies he had lost track.
So Jack had to bake
A large carrot cake
So the bunnies would all hop back.

Knock, Knock!

Who's there?

Howard

Howard who?

Howard you like some carrot stew?

FUN FACTS IT'S TRUE.

Carrots have been around for hundreds of years. What you might not know is that carrots were not always orange. Believe it or not, early carrots were purple and red. At one time, this colorful vegetable had many different uses. Carrots were first grown to use in medicine.

Scream for Ice Cream

What's a ghost's favorite dessert?

Boo-berries and I-scream.

Knock, Knock!

Who's there?

Wheel

Wheel who?

Wheel you share an ice cream with me?

How do you make an elephant float?

Two scoops of ice cream, some root beer, and an elephant!

Once known as "iced cream," the dessert was shortened to "ice cream" by American colonists. Did you know that ice cream started as ice mixed with fruit or toppings like honey? Over the years, ice cream has changed. Today's ice cream is made with ingredients like milk, cream, sugar, and flavoring.

IT'S TRUE.

There was a young lady with eyes
That got bigger and bigger in size
When she spied a dessert
That appeared to be dirt
But tasted like ice cream surprise.

Knock, Knock!

Who's there?

Tanks

Tanks who?

Tanks for the ice cream sundae with a cherry on top!

Five frozen fruity pops

What happens to ice cream cones who fight?

They get licked.

Why did the ice cream cone become a reporter?

To get the latest scoop.

There was an old man who said, "Wow!
I can't finish my dessert right now,
Or my oversized load
Will need to be towed,
And my wife will think I'm a cow."

Did you hear that the ice cream parlor closed?

Yeah, I heard that sundaes wouldn't work on weekdays, the ice cream bars went nuts, and the bananas split.

I scream, you scream, we all scream for ice cream!

Knock, Knock!

Who's there?

Les

Les who?

Les go to the ice cream parlor!

FUN FACTS

IT'S TRUE.

What is your favorite dessert? If you answered "ice cream," you are probably not alone.

Did you know that ice cream was among George Washington's favorite foods? That's right. George Washington loved ice cream so much he often served it to his guests.

Sandy sits scooping six scoops of ice cream with a skinny spoon.

Write Your Own Knock-Knock Jokes

Knock-knock jokes use a play on words to tell a funny story. You can write your own knock-knock jokes. It's very simple. First, think of a theme for your joke. For example, you might choose to write a joke about animals. Next, start off with the basic beginning for a knock-knock joke.

Knock, knock.

Who's there?

Then add a creative word or name like this:

Justin.

Then ask:

Justin who?

Finally, think of a punch line that ties in with your theme, in this case, animals. You might write something like this:

Justin time to walk my dog.

Now try writing a knock-knock joke of your own!

Words to Know

joke—Something that is said that makes you laugh.

limerick—A funny poem that is usually five lines, where lines 1, 2, and 5 rhyme, and lines 3 and 4 rhyme.

mineral—A substance found in foods needed daily to keep our bodies healthy.

nectar—A sweet liquid from flowers used by bees to make honey.

nutrients—Healthy ingredients.

orchards—Farms where fruit trees are grown.

pollination—The process of transferring pollen to the same flower or to another flower.

riddle—A puzzling question that you guess the answer to.

tongue twister—Fun words that when put together can be hard to say.

vitamin—A substance found in food that is needed for good health.

Read More

Books

Chmielewski, Gary. *Let's Eat in the Funny Zone: Jokes, Riddles, Tongue Twisters, and "Daffynitions."* Chicago, Ill.: Norwood House Press, 2008.

Phillips, Bob. *Good Clean Knock-Knock Jokes for Kids.* Eugene, Ore.: Harvest House Publishers, 2007.

Super Clean Jokes for Kids. Uhrichsville, Ohio: Barbour Publishing, 2009.

Weitzman, Ilana, Eva Blank, Rosanne Green, and Alison Benjamin. *Jokelopedia: The Biggest, Best, Silliest, Dumbest Joke Book Ever.* New York: Workman Publishing Company, 2006.

Internet Addresses

Jokes for Kids
< http://www.activityvillage.co.uk/kids_jokes.htm >

NIEHS Kids' Pages: Jokes and Trivia
< http://kids.niehs.nih.gov/jokes.htm >

Index

A
apples, 8–11
Appleseed, Johnny, 9
Aztec Indians, 30

B
bees, 25, 26, 27, 28
berry, 4, 6, 7
butter, 17–20

C
cacao tree, 13
carrots, 37–40
Chapman, John, 9
chocolate, 12–16
colonists, 42

E
eggs, 21–24

F
fats, 18
food pyramid, 23

H
hen, 22, 23
honey, 25–28

I
ice cream, 41–44

K
kernel, 32
King Tut, 25

L
La Tomatina Festival, 34

M
Mexico, 30
minerals, 22, 38

O
orchards, 10

P
Pilgrims, 9
popcorn, 29–32
protein, 23

S
Spain, 34
strawberries, 4–7

T
tomatoes, 33–36
tongue twister, 6

V
vitamins, 22, 38

W
Washington, George, 44

Y
yolk, 21, 22